DEVIL'S LAKE

BY

SARAH M. SALA

TOLSUN PUBLISHING, INC.
FLAGSTAFF, ARIZONA & LAS VEGAS, NEVADA

Devil's Lake

Copyright © 2020 by Sarah M. Sala. All rights reserved. Printed in the United States of America. First Edition. For more information, contact Tolsun Books at info@tolsunbooks.com.

Edited by Risa Papas.

Cover art by Meesh Nah.
Cover design by David Pischke and Brandi Pischke.

Set in Freight Text Pro 10 pt font.
Design by David Pischke.

ISBN 978-1-948800-37-2

Published by Tolsun Publishing, Inc.
Flagstaff, Arizona & Las Vegas, Nevada
www.tolsunbooks.com

For CQ,
the love of my life

&

For Mom, Dad, Cat, Bethany, and Christin,
my ride or die family

TABLE OF CONTENTS

III.

I am out with lanterns, looking for myself.

—Emily Dickinson

HYDROGEN

You wanna talk BANG? Hydrogen was there at 0:00 hours
in the coke-colored velodrome of dark matter.
Gasses checking gasses ad infinitum—chartreuse flare
then a deafening birth: ions of cosmos cartwheeling pink
red yellow green purple blue black in the sphere of night.
First I was a star, then a stain of water, then a kindergartner.

I.

NATURE VS. NATURE

After Leeanne Maxey

Before I was born

my original face[1]

radiated light

weather, organisms

landforms, celestial

bodies[2]   _____[3]

  everything

untouched   by humans

---

1. was queer (too)
2. unbound by
3. Nature

Aubade

Sometimes when my love and I lay senseless
in the woolpack of sleep, I recall the *coma*: nebulous cloud
of ice and dust sublimating the nucleus of a comet—

and it becomes the fuzz of a workday burned up in commuter traffic
or lost in the Oort Cloud of meetings. When my partner
steps out for work, I get a twinge of loss. Then comes

the plush feeling of domesticity, that infinite fish turning inside me.
On the same night as the Charleston Church Shooting,
I listen to a scientist's recording of a plant dying of thirst.

It sounds like the first drops of rain striking an air conditioner,
then a torrential downpour. In America, it's possible
for a white supremacist to sit in a prayer meeting for an hour,

then kill nine black parishioners. The living ask:
Where do we go to get free? Where do we go to live?
The human heart weighs only as much as a can of Coke.

Before *Much Ado About Nothing*

When I read a poem
that fucks me up
with its gorgeousness
I don't want to be the poet.
I want to be the poem.
I'm sorry for bumping
into your mom, Kid.
It was summer in NYC.
Little white face, you
craned back your head
to face the accuser.
In the afterlife, I'll be
a poem. Just a plain
sheet of typing paper
bludgeoned with ink.
The one that captures
the tar-green tenderness
in your eyes, hardened
with daughterly outrage.

BLUE DOG

Mid-sentence while teaching
a freshman seminar, a stranger

in a blue dog costume enters.
Blue Dog paces in eerily

without saying a word—
mimes his threadbare mitts

for us to carry-on. I search
the shadowbox of mesh

beneath its battered plastic eyes
for any indication of what's next.

Where an ID card should rest,
an empty plastic case swings.

When Blue Dog speaks,
his voice is crushed gravel:

One time I buried a bone.
I buried a bone, then I dug it up.

A part of me leaves my body.
When it's over, he walks out.

Five days later, an Oregon community
college student shoots his English teacher

and nine others. The gunman says,
I've wanted to do this for years.

On My Back
After Leeanne Maxey

American insults lie in the body.
They flail across the knife.
I study the green air plants

threaded across a chain link fence—
the matchsticks of your life
startled clean and blazing.

Observe a palate of flesh tones
disappear into starless denim:
reduction its own form of bloodshed.

So much depends upon the landscape
before its wildness leeches away.
The viewer's assumptions thrown

back at her. As if to say,
my queerness is the most
natural thing I inhabit.

AMERICAN AMMUNITION

With our revolutionary "Safe Action" trigger system, the G17 9x19 pistol is safe, easy, and quick— just what you need in high-pressure situations.
—glock.com

1.

A public cafeteria, the ghost of my heart gorges herself on spent ammunition.

The Orlando medical examiner processed each of the 49 Pulse victims apart from the gunman. Even amid gravitational collapse, surviving atoms couldn't reanimate with him.

2.

I forget my hands in the grocery store. Ten ringed digits in a bed of brussels sprouts. My voice becomes a skateboard ramp. Weather balloons eclipse my eyes.

Sudden questions plague me: What is a border crossing? What longitude and latitude in the cosmos do our loved ones recycle toward?

3.

Empty classrooms become scenarios. I am a cartographer of stairwells, an apostle of pony walls.

A ghost appears seeking household items. Pauses before the nightstand. Opens the drawer to rifle past hand creams, nail files, paperback books. *Over here*, I say. *Are you my afterlife?*

4.

In a dream, I ward off the shooter with blossoms: //cobalt// //fuchsia// //burnt orange// //mustard// //turquoise// //lime// //mallard// //gargoyle// //snow// //oyster// //bourbon//

A carpet of fragrance to barricade the steel doors.

A Rainstorm Reminded Me Why I Love

When I heard *wife*, my belly went reverent with breath. I was organizing upholstery swatches when the sky broiled the streets in an ancient lake of steam. I sensed your body bed down beside mine on a cool night and it left me full and wanting. Kissing you felt like the shiver of athletic prowess sideswiped by the pleasure of language. Marriage equality didn't exist until a year into our marriage. We weren't going to abandon our attractions, but swerve into them.

People I Love Tell Me To Hurry And Get Married

1.

Today I googled how to spell *thigh*,
as if the muscular ancestors inside

my jeans were mistranslations of longing.
Longing to be found, then found, again.

When I have kids, I'll carry my wife's eggs.
The question becomes, who adopts at birth?

Does CQ sign for her genetic instruction?
From the cosmos sparked in my womb

how can a signature draw love nearer?

2.

Last night I dreamed I was teaching a class

on horror stories. It was the closest to joy
I'd felt since being laid off. In the lecture,

inside the dream, it grew harder to inhale.
Pain-brain broke in calmly: *wake up*

fire sale climate shift profit loss
you are having an asthma attack.

At the end of the world, there is only
whom you loved and how you treated them.

Poem After Man

1.

I thought here's a man. Who owns who he is.
Look how natural you move in your animal skin.

2.

Paraffin wax burns at a steady rate of 0.1 g/min, releasing roughly 80 watts.
Low light, we touched each other's faces and shoulders, softened into the quilt.
A dark-furred skyscraper loomed at the window, waiting to be let in to sleep alongside his masters.

4

My   mother   //laughs// interrupts everything to unbottle hilarity.

You like him as much as a kitchen table?

3.

If we married/ I would decade you/ in the kitchen/ our children's bright specs/ traces of stray crayon/ adorn/ your spalted grooves/ stay while the baby/ sleeps with you cheek/ to cheek/ pendant dreams of the bluegrey seas/ we were born to planet earth/ to our mothers/ and grew from seed.

"I apologize if you thought this was some kind of trajectory," she said.

"Maple," he said.

In the coffee shop, I explained I felt about our male co-worker the same way I did a kitchen table.

Rapped my knuckles on the wood grain our lattes scraped across.

Her hand brushed my thigh.

I joked that if a bus took him out,
I'd just make new weekend plans.

Soon, I baked a plethora of scones to sate her.

I went in entertaining the idea of men, and left certain women are the reason we toil at all.

WOMAN

This is how to watch a man's hands while reading a novel. This is how to interpret his smudged undershirt for auspice. This is how you monitor the subway car empty from Manhattan to Brooklyn. This is how his glassy brown eyes take interest in you. This is how to erase your face, align your back, position your legs to meld into the r160 subway bench. This is how to prepare to run while casually seated. This is how he detonates the space between you. This is the separate exit you take. This is how you terrorize a woman. This is how to be polite.

STONE (BUTCH)

After Leeanne Maxey

I'm feeling myself today/ stonewash jeans that flaunt me/ in all the right places/ Casual western shirt/ pearled buttons/ sleeves cuffed at the elbow/ boots laced tight against the day/ I sing myself into the world/ not as mirror but mineral/ more intensifying adjective/ than butcher/ The square root of time/ follows the increase in the earth's mantle/ Who wouldn't want to be a secret? A van full of history/ parked in a dark movie theater/ Also implied, sense of testicle/ A stone absorbs light/ but this in turn generates heat/ A woman kisses me so hard/ she breaks/ her own front tooth/ The way she tells it I become a beer bottle

On Recieving a Homophobic Letter: a series of erasures
Version I

My Dear ▮

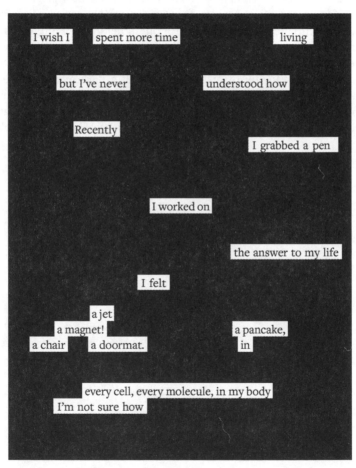

I wish I spent more time living

but I've never understood how

Recently

I grabbed a pen

I worked on

the answer to my life

I felt

a jet
a magnet!
a chair a doormat. a pancake,
in

every cell, every molecule, in my body
I'm not sure how

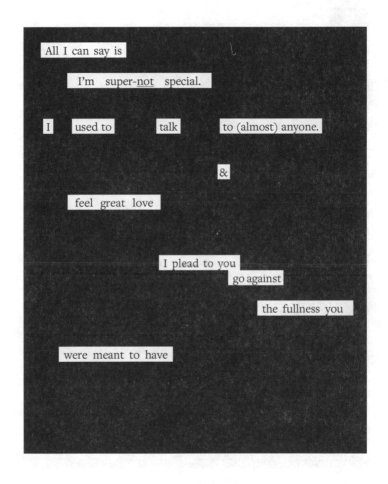

All I can say is

I'm super-<u>not</u> special.

I used to talk to (almost) anyone.

&

feel great love

I plead to you
go against

the fullness you

were meant to have

Version II

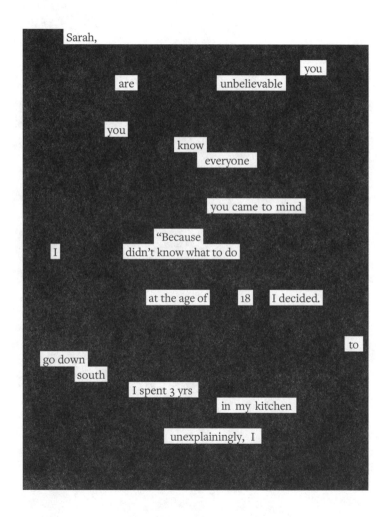

Sarah,

you

are   unbelievable

you

know
everyone

you came to mind

"Because
didn't know what to do

I

at the age of   18   I decided.

to

go down
south

I spent 3 yrs

in my kitchen

unexplainingly, I

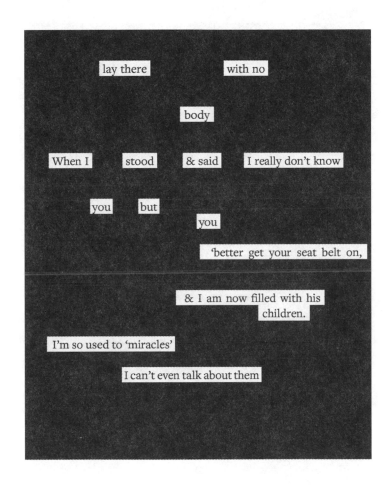

VERSION III

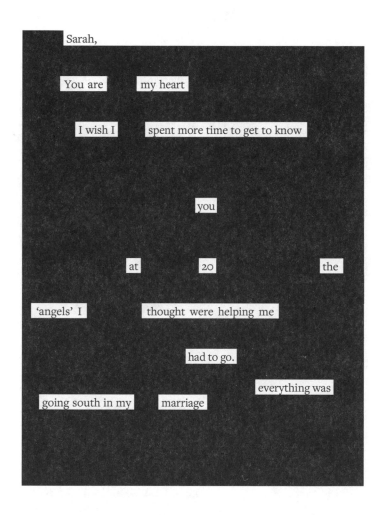

Sarah,

You are   my heart

I wish I   spent more time to get to know

you

at   20   the

'angels' I   thought were helping me

had to go.

everything was

going south in my   marriage

24

I was in a jet blast w/no feeling

I'm not sure how long it was.

you're

turning a new page

I feel great love for you

you are   my heart

                        you   you
        you

ATTENDANCE: A CATALOGUE OF ABSENCES: my car broke down, my mother became someone I didn't recognize, I had a relapse, my sister got beat up, I felt the tremendous anxiety of living, do you remember me, no busses go there, I had an abortion, I'm bedridden with a virus, my ex-boyfriend robbed me, the nurses are sweet, I couldn't find parking, one of my animals died and the other is sick, I fell asleep and didn't wake up, my grandma is having a mastectomy, we're pulling the plug on my aunt today, I had to pick up my rat from the vet, a power surge broke all the light bulbs in my house, Twitter released my home address, I miss the numbness sometimes, I'm driving my mother to work, I'm sliding in the snow, I got a speeding ticket, I went snowboarding, I'm in holding, my my ankle is broken, I didn't understand the assignment.

TANAGER STREET

Home after dark
I listen for the electric
whine of the television,
for her slipper shuffle.

I wait to hear the tumble
of clothes in the dryer,
the kettle whistle
from the stove.

Not even a vacuum
disturbs the silence.
I am late and want
to be forgiven.

II.

A Study in Plants

After Leeanne Maxey

What is it about greenery
that makes it yours?

A looking, a portal,
a universe of green

inlaid over a tapestry
of grass. How can

you tell a lesbian
from everyone else?

NATURE POEM

SP 4.217 (9-70)

PENNSYLVANIA STATE POLICE
EVIDENCE *Gettysburg*

STATION:

CODE | INVENTORY NO.
2/60 | 2860 "0"

OFFENSE: *Murder*

DATE OCCURRED: 5-13-88

INCIDENT NO.: H6-487099

LOCATION:

VICTIM: *Rebecca P. Wight*

SUSPECT:

ACCUSED:

COLLECTED BY: *Blevins*

BADGE NO.:

DATE: 5-14-88

In 1988, Claudia Brenner and her girlfriend, Rebecca Wight, planned to hike a section of the remote Appalachian Trail in Pennsylvania. They encountered a stranger who shot them both, killing Rebecca.

32

Little loop

trail rocky

outcrop

where

dark   earth

verged

with wild

azaleas

The moss

spongy,

but wet

your lips

straddled mine,

an eager

cloudberry

My bicep

exploded   then,

the dirt

Earthquake?

Volcano?

Landslide?

Bright red

spatter on

our green

tent cover

A volcano

does not

make you

bleed

Our bodies

soft targets

along

the riverbank

Because I ran

first, he knew

to expect

you

.22 ammo

perfect for

small game

The fifth bullet

tore a   wormhole

in my pharynx

the seventh

ruptured   your

liver

Leaving us

for dead:

        He said,

I wanted

to join in

I wrapped

the blue

sleeping bag

around you

birds still

loud in

the trees

Later,

I passed

a girl seated

in a sunflower

field

I knew it

was you even if

you were

gone

Four miles

I forged

a trail

to the

highway

A white

towel

plugged

my exit

wounds

Finally,

a wide

forestry road

a car full

of teenage boys

ferried me

away

Rebecca,

your parents

cremated you

before I left

the hospital

When I Was A Boy

It was always summer// we brandished unripe chests
to launch stunt bikes over gaping foundations.

Our dirty fingers tendered past thorns to wolf
blackberries from the shade of weeping willows.

Sequined snakes curled toward us in the lake
like nightmares we procrastinated with rocks.

A recess monitor called: *keep your coats on unless
you're wearing an undershirt.* Suddenly, it was spring.

A boy presumed sameness to peer down my sweater.
At first, I was a boy\\ then I became a rosebud.

III.

MRI REVEALS

little bladder inside a switch board
of grey matter

what can I name that measures 7.5 cm?

crayon wrapper
credit card
half a $20 bill
the span of my palm

tiny animal, I
just a bundle of cells
inside my mother

sly balloon,
it took you 29 years to fill

then another 3 to press
into the tall grasses of my words

it's all very abstract
like trying to imagine

a quasar beneath the dura
of my skull

No One Ever Asked Me If I Liked Being Called Pluto

When Pluto was a planet, Z got detention for keeping
their eyes open during prayer. They wondered, are all
grandmas named Dorothy? Their mind became a voice

no one else could hear. When no one knew what a planet
was anymore, Z read the Sunday comics alongside
the original eight. New mnemonics replaced the old:

They love me, they're terrestrial. They love me not,
they're gaseous. They love me, I'm an ice planet.
Z studied childhood obesity with jelly beans asking,

which one is the best? When Pluto was a dwarf planet,
Z had sex in a pajama set, with the Kuiper Belt repeating
yes-yes-yes-yes. Children wrote misspelled letters

to scientists exclaiming, *if there are poeple who live*
there they won't exist. Then Z's sister birthed a niece,
a small impact with jet black hair. They named her Lola.

SYMPATHETIC HEADACHE

1.

When I talk of incompatible elements, I mean before Gameboys
and battery lust, cadmium was just a particle tracing a coal miner's
parted lip. Slender 0.1 dusting in the Earth's Crust—
can you *dig* it? Now I'm the blue and green phosphors
in Miley Cyrus's genderqueer color television. *No, we can't stop.*
No, we won't stop electroplating with abandon.

2.

There are no stores
on the moon. Only the
dark centers of the lunar maria.

Missing you isn't so bad.
Thinking about you makes me happy,
the astronaut read from
a crumpled postcard tucked
into her suit.

Early scientists bet their wives
these craters held seas.

An impossible woman
stood on her porch
in Texas.

A dark speck
absorbing the pour
of refrigerator light
from the moon.

Like a fly heavy with cold,
battening down the
latches on the sheep pens.

3.

On film,
my very
own rotator
cuff,
frayed fibers
of labrum,
wisp of wool,

white

signal

amid

black signal.

My undoing:
the careless
whim
of a
dandelion
spur.

The Image Surprises

Great-grandmother with nightwater black hair
braided down her back

Aunt who learned at her mother's funeral
the Native tribes we descended from   now losing
photons of her brain to dementia

Blood isn't culture—

If it were, I'd know how to prepare
a Polish New Year's feast:
a lucky silver fish

My other great-grandmother donated her body
to science in Detroit   Returned in 1987
as an urn we kept in the closet
beside the board games

Whenever I stole inside for hide-and-seek,
or a blanket, I whispered *hello*

Lots of people think I only have
two sisters. But there's a third—

I used to joke *I'm not gay my girlfriend is*
Until a priest advised my sister
to absent my wedding

Now I carry a picture of her
like a missing persons report
I could file at any moment

So, I try to tell you a story:
It's easier to say a man
loved blue so much

he married a blueberry
and rolled her all the way
to France

Than it is to say sequence
is a binding thread. And we're
all just trying not to spin off
into the moon

Blake

Last night I ate a bowl of venison stew
and tasted Michigan's sweet grass.

I learned to sight a shotgun before
my first period, and pheasant-hunted

just once: rambled for hours through
the tall brush, willing the jade birds

not to startle skyward. Blake was buried
with a veil shrouding his face.

The bullet's pressure wave a battering
ram against the bright moon of his skull.

When I think of Blake, I see two men
twist aluminum pylons into the muck,

then heft docks onto crossbars for us
to walk on water. When a sniper fires

a round he accounts for the Coriolis
effect: the earth rotates under the shot,

shifting the target away. My dad listens
patiently and offers no answers, moves

to the driveway to wash his truck.
Works the wheels until they gleam.

60-Year Slide

I said, "Sweetheart, the water's already been off."
—Nicole Hill

A pipe wrench
tempers serrated teeth
    that bite with
    increasing
    brutality as
    it turns

-*-

    When she
    came to die,
    Dorothy did
    not bring her
    birding books.
    As a young
    woman, it
    was agonizing
    to pretend
    the doctor's
    restriction—
    six ounces
    of water, per
    hour—
    was not
    torture.

-*-

Tell me the story of Detroit/ The fear mongering debt crisis/ "Grand Bargain"
art heist at the DIA/ an INTERACTIVE MAP OF 3,400 HOMES/ SLATED
FOR DEMOLITION/
                    Little Hamtramck house/ where my father was born/
            clot of red blood cells/ now a googlemap of blight/ seat me
        in the ghost/ assembly line where/ Richard stood/ a semicentury
cutting steel/ FORD MOTOR COMPANY/ his four boys/ hawked for college

        -*-

        Race red
        steel, 48 in.
        reinforced
        handle, full
        floating
        forged hook
        jaw. Tail
        pierced
        with a grommet
        for hanging
        when not
        in use.

                                -*-
            You watch a woman   die,
            of thirst,   it changes you.

Epigrams For Dorothy

i am the maine coon
you drowned in iron
lake

a fisherman crashed
in after you
but i got held under

were you trying to drown yourself
in the lake & needed the cat?
did you see the fisherman?
he never saw the cat

i am the persian feline
you call kitty-doggie

i don't care what you call me
i won't come near you

on visits i wriggled
deep into the fresh down
weft of your comforter

a jolly clam
of teeth swam beside
us in a jar

you haven't phoned
a soul in seven years
i am your ears

it's me, meeko!
the shitzu you put down
i'm waiting on the other side
will you bring gumdrops?

we are the letters
your granddaughter wrote.
we lined the pockets
of your winter coat
the bottom of your purse

i am your neighbor lady
from iron lake. our kids
used to play together
now we're roommates
in a nursing home
& we don't know it

Manitou Beach: A Duet

Little s was baptized
A phobia is a memory
in Devil's Lake
passed down
at the foot of her
for generations
parents' cottage

> Little s inscribed her
> *Her entire life*
> naked body with lipstick
> *people who love her*
> before a bath. Thought
> *will leave her*
> no one would ever
> *for nature*
> catch her

Big B parked her (three kids)
Master of shy courage
and a shopping cart
the first time little s made
at the Meijer Grocery
herself bold

A lady walked by, remarked
You said, because we are
those look like Big B's kids
and identified yourself

Little B loomed defiant,
The planets were dark that night.
a milk tooth suddenly larger
Big B bathed her, face stony like a Greek letter
than any sibling rivalry

Little B bit her own forearm
Their Venus. Their Goblin of delight
with the single tooth in her gums
A very naughty child

One winter Big S broke
floundered before
through the ice—
materializing
ragged aperture
electrified with feeling

The first time Big B laughed
This pill wouldn't
was accidental
take a headache away
A migraine: one Tylenol
from a— from a—
stuck in the bottle

A goose! you hollered. Big B laughed
This special feeling of ability,
with newly shaped eyes
a particle accelerator
Eyebrows high on her head

C was older. She could read the comics

Without warning or intention

Little s and C strolled onto the dock

The anger that defined them

Without warning or intention

This earliest misunderstanding

C crashed into the lake in her party outfit

Like two knives sharpening each other

Torpedoed up sputtering

Two sisters born on the same day

three years apart

Government cheese. Velveeta orange!

You never remember it better

Rectangular box for cards

than you do the car ride home

Little b. Greatest of all time (G.O.A.T)

A case of cheese. Three pounds of cheese

A tank full of responsibility

So much cheese pinning your legs to the seat

EARTH 2018

Now, when the planet made its efforts to break free
a FedEX employee discovered M77232917—
the largest prime number ever decoded.

Scientists mined ice on Mars: bands of snow dating
back a million years, discovered Earth's lost eighth
continent, and seven new planets in the Goldilocks Zone:

neither too hot nor too cold to sustain life.
Other disasters that now seem miserable: elections,
wildfires, mud slides, and influenzas—

humans did not let rain, floating night, or tomorrow
stop Earth's leave going. Consumption,
the naked invader we mistook for king.

Rothko's Chapel

A spaceship to map grief's occipital orbit// A bloodstone door

If I had a choice, I would teach the politicians art

Or the words: sauce, poison, and praise

The self is a verb when the mundane fails solace

If I had a choice: a comet-riddled night

A purple pheasant ascending

A double-hung window set ablaze

If I had a choice, a two-lane highway

A way out of the furnace

Untraceable

The last thing you said to me
was if you do this, I'll never speak
to you again. Until today, I could imagine
your life. Now my daydreams occur in careful,
calculated measure. Late afternoon naps
at my desk chair, head tipped back, it's safe
to conjure your bright smile. As if somehow
by focusing on a tooth, I can't be torn by it.
I remember your body, politely. Chaste praise
of the curve of your buttock rounding into thigh.
Idiot memory, mine, it's no longer my right to chronicle.
Yet the dark nettles of your frankness have softened
into daydreams of old care packages.
Is this how love ends? A gradual
retirement of the lead hammer
dug into a trench in the seashore.
I say love never leaves us completely.
I say, in gratitude of this life,
I wish a thousand kindnesses on you.
Untraceable, back to me.

Interior vs. Exterior

At my worst, I control the boundaries of my form, and yet, when divine, the self permeates the physical world. It's true the atoms of our bodies grieve each other in death just like a color doesn't occur alone—but takes meaning from other colors. The moon was a changeable star that ruled men's fate. Water was green and not blue to medieval cartographers. The complexity of ochre begs the viewer to grapple with it. We are swiftly becoming an indoor species. Yet, scientists know more about outer space than the Earth's oceans. Humans brought the natural world into their homes to combat the rise of machines. Without us knowing, trees converse via latticed fungi. Gender isn't something one is, but performs. We are a vast assembly of nerve cells—the continents longing for each other.

Acknowledgements

Grateful acknowledgement is made to the editors where poems in *Devil's Lake* first appeared, often in earlier versions:

The Ghost Assembly Line Finishing Line Press New Women's Voices Chapbook Series, Belt Publishing's *LGBTQ Anthology, The Antigonish Review, Atlas Review, Bodega Magazine, BOMB, First Class Literary Magazine, Foglifter Journal, Impakter, Leveler, The Los Angeles Review, The Mackinac, New Poetry From the Midwest Anthology, No,Dear, The Oleander Review, Poetry Ireland Review, San Diego Reader, The Southampton Review, The Stockholm Review of Literature, SWWIM, Tinderbox Poetry Journal, Universal Oneness Anthology: an Anthology of Magnum Opus Poems From Around the World, Vending Machine Press, Women Studies Quarterly* (WSQ), *Wreck Park.*

Devil's Lake was a finalist for the 2017 Subito Book Prize and the 2019 New Issues Press Poetry Prize. Profound thanks to these presses for their recognition.

Special thanks to Risa Pappas, Geoffrey Nutter, and Catherine Barnett for your keen editorial prowess.

Deep gratitude to all of my teachers and mentors, especially: CAConrad, Anselm Berrigan, Anne Carson, Laura Kasischke, Myung Mi Kim, Aric Knuth, Deborah Landau, Raymond McDaniel, Gregory Pardlo, Meghan O'Rourke, Matthew Rohrer, Charles Simic, Suzanne Spring, and Keith Taylor.

Sincerest thanks to the Office Hours Poetry Fellows for your incredible feedback and unparalleled community. Thank you to the 2019 Poets House Emerging Poets Workshop for your inspiring presence and rad poems.

Many thanks to friends, editors, and colleagues: Rabih Ahmed, Raluca Albu, Kiran Bath, Abba Belgrave, Chris Caldemeyer, Nicole Callihan, Carrie Hohmann-Campbell, Catherine Chen, Kate Conroy, Marty Correia, Laura Cresté, Patrick Delorey, Elizabeth Devlin, Linda Harris-Dolan, Thomas Dooley, Ralph Emrick, Charlene François, Tripp Grilli, Sophie Herron, Aimee Herman, Emily Hockaday, Jen Hyde, Mara Jebsen, Trevor Ketner, Jen Levitt, Shalewa Mackall, Ricardo Alberto Maldonado, Paco Márquez, Leeanne Maxey, Caitlin McDonnell, Missy Mende, Amy Meng, Brandon Menke, Holly Mitchell, James Fujinami Moore, Madeleine Mori, Jerome Ellison Murphy, Joe Pan, Val Rigodon, Noel Sikorski, Aldrin Valdez, and Nicole Wallace.

I am wonderfully indebted to the Tolsun Books Family for your dedication and vision on this project: Risa Pappas, David Pischke, Brandi Pischke, and Heather Lang-Cassera.

Thank you to "The Band" for giving me life when I need it most: David Ignell, Kristy Jackson, and Craig Dudnynskii Aloo, to my marathon and breakfast burrito partners, Bert Chantarat and John Kelly.

Immense thanks to my wusband, CQ. I admire your big bold dreams, and love you madly.

NOTES

"Aubade"

Where do we go to get free? Where do we go to live? is quoted from Jessica Lynne and DéLana R.A. Dameron's interview at ARTS.BLACK.

"Stone (Butch), On My Back, nature vs. Nature, & A Study in Plants"

are all inspired by Leeanne Maxey paintings.

"Nature Poem"

is inspired by Claudia Brenner's memoir, *Eight Bullets: One Woman's Story of Surviving Anti-Gay Violence* (Firebrand Books 1995), and the short film *In the Hollow* directed by Austin Bunn. Some lines are adapted from Claudia Brenner's interview transcript via the Rare Books and Manuscripts holdings at Cornell University.

"Nobody Ever Asked if I Liked Being Called Pluto"

If there are poeple who live there, they won't exist is quoted from the article, "6 Angry Letters Kids Sent Neil deGrasse Tyson About Pluto" by Lucas Reilly via *Mental Floss*.

SARAH M. SALA is a poet, educator, and native Michigander with degrees from the University of Michigan and New York University. She is the recipient of fellowships from Poets House, The Ashbery Home School, and Sundress Academy for the Arts. Her work appears in *BOMB, Poetry Ireland Review, Michigan Quarterly Review,* and *The Southampton Review,* among others. The founding director of Office Hours Poetry Workshop, and assistant poetry editor for the *Bellevue Literary Review,* she teaches expository writing at New York University and lives in Washington Heights with her wusband. www.sarahsala.com.